Sometimes I think
Perchance that Allah
                may
When he created Cats,
    have thrown away
The Tails he marred in
        making, and they grew
To Cat Tails and to
    Pussy Willows grey

                Oliver Herford

The
Rubáiyát
of a
Persian Kitten

By

Oliver Herford

Gramercy Books
NEW YORK • AVENEL

This 1993 edition is published by Gramercy Books,
distributed by Outlet Book Company, Inc.
a Random House Company,
40 Engelhard Avenue
Avenel, New Jersey 07001

Random House
New York • Toronto • London • Sydney • Auckland

Cover design by Debra Borg

Printed and bound in the United States of America

Library of Congress Cataloging in Publication Data
Herford, Oliver, 1863-1935.
The Rubaiyat of a Persian kitten / written and illustrated
by Oliver Herford.
p.   cm.
ISBN 0-517-09305-7
1. Persian cat—Poetry.   2. Cats—Poetry.   I. Title.
PS3511.E62R8   1993b
811'.52—dc20   93-779
                                      CIP

8 7 6 5 4 3 2 1

The Rubáiyát of a
Persian Kitten

Wake! for the Golden Cat has
           put to flight
The Mouse of Darkness
           with his Paw of Light:
Which means, in Plain and
           simple every-day
Unoriental Speech—The Dawn
           is bright.

They say the Early Bird the
     Worm shall taste.
Then rise, O Kitten! Wherefore,
       sleeping, waste
The fruits of Virtue? Quick!
      the Early Bird
Will soon be on the flutter—O
       make haste!

The Early Bird has gone, and
    with him ta'en
The Early Worm—Alas! the
                Moral 's plain,
O Senseless Worm!   Thus,
            thus we are repaid
for Early Rising—I shall doze
                again.

The Mouse makes merry 'mid
    the Larder Shelves,
The Bird for Dinner in the
                Garden delves.
   I often wonder what the
                creatures eat
One half so toothsome as they
                are Themselves.

And that Inverted Bowl of
        Skyblue Delf
That helpless lies upon the
                    Pantry Shelf—
    Lift not your eyes to It for
                    help, for It
Is quite as empty as you are
                    yourself.

The Ball no question makes of
                Ayes or Noes,
But right or left, as strikes the
                                Kitten, goes;
Yet why, altho' I toss it far
                                Afield,
It still returneth—Goodness
                only knows!

A Secret Presence that my
         likeness feigns,
And yet, quicksilver-like, eludes
                           my pains—
    In vain I look for Him
                behind the glass;
    He is not there, and yet He still
                        remains.

What out of airy Nothing to
        invoke
A senseless Something to resist
                the stroke
Of unpermitted Paw—upon
                the pain
Of Everlasting Penalties—if
                broke.

I sometimes think the Pussy-
        Willows grey
Are Angel Kittens who have lost
                their way,
And every Bulrush on the
                river bank
A Cat-Tail from some lovely
                Cat astray.

Sometimes I think perchance
        that Allah may,
When he created Cats, have
                        thrown away
The Tails He marred in
            making, and they grew
To Cat-Tails and to Pussy-
                        Willows grey.

And lately, when I was not
	feeling fit,
Bereft alike of Piety and Wit,
	There came an Angel Shape
			and offered me
A fragrant Plant and bid me
			taste of it.

'Twas that reviving Herb, that Spicy Weed,
    The Cat-Nip. Tho' 'tis good in time of need,
Ah, feed upon it lightly, for who knows
To what unlovely antics it may lead.

Strange—is it not?—that of the numbers who
Before me passed this Door of Darkness thro',
Not one returns thro' it again, altho'
Ofttimes I 've waited here an hour or two.

'Tis but a Tent where takes
      his one Night's Rest
A Rodent to the Realms of
            Death address'd,
When Cook, arising, looks for
            him and then—
Baits, and prepares it for
            another Guest.

They say the Lion and the
      Lizard keep
The Courts where Jamshýd
      gloried and drank deep.
The Lion is my cousin; I
      don't know
Who Jamshýd is—nor shall it
      break my sleep.

Impotent glimpses of the
   Game displayed
Upon the Counter—temptingly
             arrayed;
Hither and thither moved or
       checked or weighed,
And one by one back in the Ice
          Chest laid.

What if the Sole could fling
the Ice aside,
And with me to some Area's
haven glide—
Were 't not a Shame, were 't
not a shame for it
In this Cold Prison crippled to
abide?

Some for the Glories of the
        Sole, and Some
Mew for the proper Bowl of
                Milk to come.
Ah, take the fish and let your
                Credit go,
And plead the rumble of an
                empty Tum.

One thing is certain: tho' this
        Stolen Bite
Should be my last and Wrath
                consume me quite,
    One taste of It within the Area
                        caught
Better than at the Table lost
                    outright.

Indeed, indeed Repentance oft
    before
I swore, but was I hungry when
                  I swore?
And then and then came Cook
       — with Hose in hand—
And drowned my glory in a
             sorry pour.

What without asking hither
        harried whence,
And without asking whither
          harried hence—
O, many a taste of that
          forbidden Sole
Must down the memory of that
            Insolence.

Heaven, but the vision of a
flowing Bowl;
And Hell, the sizzle of a frying
Sole
Heard in the hungry Darkness,
where Myself,
So rudely cast, must impotently
roll.

The Vine has a tough fibre
  which about
While clings my Being;—let the
     Canine flout
Till his Bass Voice be pitched
    to such loud key
It shall unlock the door I mew
      without.

Up from the Basement to the
  Seventh flat
I rose, and on the Crown of
     fashion sat,
And many a Ball unravelled
    by the way—
But not the Master's angry Bawl
    of "Scat!"

*T*hen to the Well of Wisdom I
—and lo!
With my own Paw I wrought to
make it flow,
And This was all the Harvest
that I reaped:
We come like Kittens and like
Cats we go.

Why be this Ink the fount of
        Wit?—who dare
Blaspheme the glistening Pen-
        drink as a snare?
A Blessing?—I should spread
        it, should I not?
And if a Curse—why, then upset
        it!—there!

A moment's Halt, a
        momentary Taste
Of Bitter, and amid the Trickling
                        Waste
I wrought strange shapes from
                Máh to Máhi, yet
I know not what I wrote, nor
                why they chased.

Now I beyond the Pale am
　　　safely past.
O, but the long, long time their
　　　　　Rage shall last,
Which, tho' they call to supper,
　　　　　I shall heed
As a Stone Cat should heed a
　　　　　Pebble cast.

And that perverted Soul
        beneath the Sky
They call the Dog—Heed not his
                angry Cry;
    Not all his Threats can make
            me budge one bit,
Nor all his Empty Bluster
                    terrify.

They are no other than a
        moving Show
Of whirling Shadow Shapes that
        come and go
Me-ward thro' Moon illumined
        Darkness hurled,
In midnight, by the Lodgers in
        the Row.

Myself when young did eagerly
          frequent
The Backyard fence and heard
                great Argument
About it, and About, yet
                    evermore
Came out with fewer fur than in
                I went.

Ah, me! if you and I could
        but conspire
To grasp this Sorry Scheme of
                things entire,
Would we not shatter it to
                bits, and then
Enfold it nearer to our Heart's
                Desire?

Tho' Two and Two make four
        by rule of line,
Or they make Twenty-two by
                        Logic fine,
Of all the figures one may
                        fathom, I
Shall ne'er be floored by anything
                        but Nine.

And fear not lest Existence
    shut the Door
On You and Me, to open it no
                    more.
The Cream of Life from out
        your Bowl shall pour
Nine times—ere it lie broken on
                the floor.

So, if the fish you Steal—the
      Cream you drink—
Ends in what all begins and ends
                in, Think,
Unless the Stern Recorder
               points to Nine,
Tho' They would drown you—
          still you shall not sink.